The Stor
Brimscom
Where Thames and Severn Met

Brimscombe, Basin.

ISBN No. 978-0-9561743-1-4
Published by the Cotswold Canals Trust, May 2010
2 Bell House, Wallbridge Lock, Stroud, Glos., GL5 3JS
Written for the Cotswold Canals Trust by Graham Hobbs
assisted by pupils from Brimscombe (C.E.) Primary School
Final edit and layout for the Cotswold Canals Trust: David Jowett 01453 755535
Print liaison: Sharon Kemmett at The Design Co-operative 01453 751778
Printed by StroudPrint 01453 764251
Front cover picture: Brimscombe Port by unknown artist
Courtesy Stroud District (Cowle) Museum
Back cover & this page: Brimscombe Port in the early 1900s

www.cotswoldcanals.com

3

Foreword

by Liz Payne, Chairman, Cotswold Canals Trust

The author and pupils of Brimscombe Primary School must be congratulated for telling the story of the transformation of a 'little hamlet surrounded by woods' into a major inland port. This very readable book tells the story from the beginning, through many ups and downs to the present day.

The Cotswold Canals Trust is dedicated to the restoration of the link between two great rivers, the Severn and the Thames, which includes plans to reinvigorate Brimscombe Port as an important part of that link.

The Trust has over 5,500 members, many of whom are actively involved in a wide variety of activities, from helping to crew trip boats and manning publicity stands around the country as well as getting hands-on experience of restoring and maintaining the canal itself.

I hope from reading this book that some of you may become interested in knowing more about the restoration of the 36 miles from Saul to Inglesham and even becoming a member.

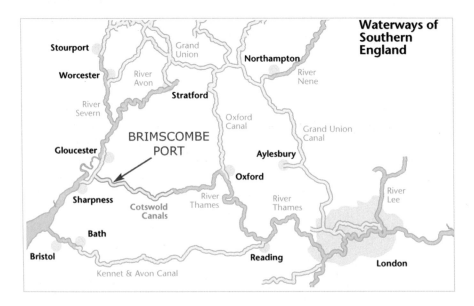

Joined Friends

Eleven big rivers in England are seen,
It starts with the Thames, the Ouse and the Nene,
The great River Humber, the Tees, Tyne and Tweed,
Leaves four to remember - that's agreed.
The Ribble, the Mersey, the Dee and the Severn,
Bring the total up to eleven.

The first river in the poem, the Thames, is the longest in England, at 215 miles while the last one, the Severn, is 219 miles making it the longest in mainland Britain. Way back in Tudor times, there was talk about linking the two but in 1641 a poet and writer actually set out to see if it could be done. He recorded his conclusions in a book, **John Taylor's Last Voyage and Adventure.** We are grateful to Cambridge University for sending us a photocopy, extracts of which pupils at Brimscombe school have transcribed. We've changed the letter which appears like an 'f' to 's' but otherwise we have stayed with Taylor's personal spelling and punctuation (or lack of it). He paddled a boat from London as far as Cirencester but from here he had to hire a cart to carry his boat and crew. During his passage on the cart he reckoned a four mile cut between the Frome springs at Bessley (Bisley) and the River Churn was all that was needed *"so Severne and Thames might be made almost ioyned friends."*

Taylor was hopelessly optimistic. When the link finally occurred, 150 years later, his suggested four mile cut needed to be ten times that distance. However, ignorant of all this, he continued his journey along the *"brooke called Stroud, with passing and wading, with haling over bankes at fulling milles (where there are many) with plucking over suncke trees, over and under strange Bridges of wood and stone, and in some places the brooke was scarce as broad as my Boate, I being oftentimes impeached with bowghes and branches of willowes and Alder Trees, which grew so thicke, hanging over and into the brooke, so that the day light or Sunne could scarce peepe through the branches, that in many places all passages were stop'd: so that I was sometimes forced to cut and hew out my way with a hatchett.."*

Walkers struggling along certain stretches of the towpath today, may wonder what's changed in nearly 400 years. Meanwhile, our explorer eventually reached the Severn and published his conclusions in a poem:

In common reason, all men must agree
That if these Rivers were made cleane and free,
One Barge, with eight poore mens industrious paines,
Would carry more than forty carts or waines,
And every Waine to draw them horses five,
And each two men or boye to guide or drive.
Charge of an hundred. horse and eighty men
With eight mens labour would be served then.
Thus men would be imployd, and horse preserv'd,
And all the country at cheape rates be serv'd.

What he meant was that eight men could haul a boat carrying a load which would otherwise need a hundred horses and eighty men if it went on carts. His idea even made the horses redundant, replacing them with men. This may seem strange to us today but the pictures opposite, some of the earliest of any canals, suggest that using men rather than animals was standard practice.

Sadly for Taylor, his book was hardly off the London presses when the English Civil War broke out and his ideas were forgotten for another hundred years. Nevertheless, the waterways were eventually cleared and shipping did manage to come up the Frome, along the stretch where he once needed an axe. Boats reached Stroud in the 1750s, using cranes to bypass the mills. This system had its limitations and an actual canal, the Stroudwater, was opened in 1779 starting from the River Severn at Framilode and terminating at Wallbridge in Stroud.

Shortly after this, the Thames - Severn link idea was revived and a surveyor, named Robert Whitworth, was given the job of working out a route to join the rivers. He delivered his conclusions at the *Kings Head* pub in Cirencester in 1782. His original handwritten report can be read in Gloucester Record Office.

Whitworth considered two possibilities. To the north, a route from Tewkesbury would pass through the Cotswold Hills, via a long tunnel, to join the River Colne and so lead to the Thames. He rejected this idea because the springs which he studied along the course didn't supply enough water so it was decided to run the canal through the Golden Valley.

Etching of St Cyr's Church, Stonehouse. Three unfortunate labourers have the job of hauling a boat while a more impressive one with four oarsmen overtakes.

Etching of a scene between Daneway and Sapperton Tunnel. Note the practice of fixing the rope to the top of the mast which reduced the tendency of the boat to pull into the bank. The man steering may have the easy job for now but he is likely to have to help leg the boat through the tunnel very soon for a tortuous four hours.

Having fixed on a route, however, there remained a problem with boat shapes and sizes. Thames boats were long, 87'6" (26.67m), and thin, 11'7" (3.5m). River Severn boats, known as trows, were shorter, 60-68' (18.25-20.75m) and wider, 15' but sometimes 20' (4.5-6 m). Trows needed to be so wide to prevent them capsizing in strong Severn tides. Their width, combined with their flat bottoms, also allowed them to run over, not dig into, the shifting sand banks.

If the canal were to accommodate both types of boat, the locks would have to be both long for Thames vessels and wide for Severn ones, making them expensive to build and wasteful of water. Anticipating this, Whitworth recommended two types of canal, a narrow one with long locks running from the Thames and a wide one with shorter locks running from the Severn. Where the two met, he proposed a port, where Thames and Severn boats could swap cargoes. The canal builders chose a site as far inland from the Severn as possible before the Cotswold hills made it too narrow to fit a port in - hence Brimscombe. The following copy from the 'New History of Gloucestershire 1779, on the shelves of Gloucester Record Office, gives us an idea of what it was like at the time.

Brimſcomb is a little hamlet in the Lower Lypiat diviſion, ſituated in a pleaſant valley, on the banks of the Froom, ſurrounded with woods, and lies in the common road between Minchin Hampton and Stroud. There is in this place an antient houſe, formerly called Bigge's Place, with clothing-mills adjoining, which was the property of the late William Dallaway, eſq; who ſerved the office of high ſheriff of this county in the year 1776, and carried on a large trade in the clothing buſineſs 'till the time of his death, in the year 1775.

One can forgive the 'antient' spelling which left the 'e' missing off 'Brimscomb' but there is clearly an error that William Dallaway served as High Sheriff for Gloucestershire in 1776, having died in 1775.

Enlarged detail of part of the well-known picture seen on the cover of this book. The men towing the boat seem to have the rope fixed by a harness.

An etching showing a type of Thames barge leaving the Coates end of Sapperton Tunnel. The mast is just being raised and the tow rope is once again fixed to the top.

The 'little hamlet' didn't stay that way for long. Everything changed with the arrival of navigators, or 'navvies'. An account of their activities was kept in a book by Sarah Butler, landlady of the *Ship Inn*. Printed in 1831, priced 2/- (10p), a copy found in the British Library reads:

"About this period, the Thames and Severn Canal, which now runs through the Vale, was being cut, and men who were employed in this work were in the habit of frequenting the 'Ship Inn'.

"After refusing to supply such as had come thither in a state of intoxication, assuring them they had taken enough, and had much better reserve their money for the claims of their families, she had been surrounded by drunken men, who, deaf to all remonstrance, and enraged by her refusal, have poured forth dreadful imprecations and threatened violence, unless she yielded to their demands."

She was *"surrounded by reprobates"* as she had to stand up to the *"turbulent passions debasing desires of the licentious and profane. From the known character of this class, the reader will not be surprised at what has been said."*

The Ship Inn today

10

Sarah dealt with problem customers by calling out the Brimscombe cottagers to remove the offenders. Sarah herself was a keen Methodist, whose members tended not to drink alcohol in those days, and even the book admits that being a pub landlady was an unlikely job for a Methodist. Nevertheless she seems to have had some success for, eventually, swearing and drunkenness became rare in the pub. The book implies this was due to her Christian influence. There again, the navvies may have moved on.

Whatever the behaviour of these navvies, the Record Office has some quotations, written by them for various jobs, showing some, at least, could read, write and add up, though maybe not spell. These men also made quite an impact on the landscape during the three years they laboured, as the maps printed on the centre pages show. Before they arrived, north of the river were an assortment of water meadows, and more cultivated areas such as *"Mr. Peach, the mill owner's garden,"* or *"Miss Shepperd's orchard."* The only road in Brimscombe was Brimscombe Lane, leading up to Minchinhampton via Brimscombe Hill. Most settled folk were mill workers or agricultural labourers.

Very soon, hedgerows, plus the fields and cultivated areas they enclosed, disappeared as the port was dug out of them. To the north was a wharf with a warehouse and offices which adjoined a substantial port manager's house. This became the company headquarters. The date on the stone above the archway read 1789. Pupils using this building as a school one and a half centuries later might well have believed that Samuel Smith, who built it, also built Gloucester gaol about this time. To the west was another wharf and warehouses and from here along the south bank ran a path along to Harrison's Mill, now known as Bourne Mill. The other main feature was the island. This was built to stop folk stealing the coal stored there and required a draw bridge to get on to it. The leat, or man-made straight section of the Frome was left as it was, to continue working the wheels of Peach's, now Port, Mill. The original wandering stream disappeared under the port and island, though its route remains on the maps today. More than two hundred years later, its course is still marked, as the old parish boundary between Minchinhampton and Bisley.

Brimscombe didn't just undergo a physical change. Large boats, never seen before, appeared in the valley, with crews from as far away as London and the Midlands. The goods that came with them became more affordable. Take the price of coal, for example, which dropped by a third. Brimscombe would certainly never be the same again.

Maps tell us a certain amount but we are fortunate that Stroud's *Museum in the Park* has a very early painting of Brimscombe Port on display and we are grateful for this print, used throughout this booklet with their kind permission.

The scene must be later than 1793, when the port headquarters, painted in on the left was built, but pre-1815, because the road running through the Golden Valley built that year, isn't shown. The artist's proportions are a bit lopsided. Compare the two little toddlers pulling a trow with a giant in it. Nevertheless, the attention to detail is excellent. The picture appears to have been painted from the roadside or, given artistic licence, from the garden of Dallaways house.

In the distance on the piece of hill where the Toadsmoor Valley joins the Golden Valley is the beautiful Queen Anne house, demolished in the 1950s. The site is now a housing estate. Bourne Bridge and mill are clearly visible at the far end of the port, little changed today. The port boundary wall, which was renovated in 2008, is a lot longer for most of the northern end has disappeared now, along with the buildings just visible behind the bridge. In front of the southern section of wall is the island, with coal on it. A building is actually on the island. Later it would house the Brimscombe iron foundry. Was it doing so already or was it just for storage?

The company headquarters are easily identified. The hexagonal front to the port manager's house and office is attached to the warehouse and there appears to be a boat moored in the little inlet at the side. There's a crane on the wharf, three boats in front and some cargo lying around but where are the workers? There seems to be only one, standing beside the crane.

The Port Mill, on the right, looks very different today, again giving a clue to the date, because it was substantially rebuilt around 1810. It's a tantalising question to ask what the buildings behind the mill are. Were they more mill buildings or were they the salt store and attached cottage? If the latter, the salt store is one of the few features of the picture that can still be seen today.

The river Frome flows along the south side of the canal from Chalford but at Brimscombe it flows as spent water from the mill down a man-made straight cut and under the canal. The exit has been painted a dull red, suggesting a brick built culvert (see front cover). There is evidence for about eight boats, though the port reputedly held over a hundred. The only obvious cargo is the pile of barrels in the trow in the foreground. How those two poor souls towing it must have envied the trow in front, with its sails in action.

Make Your Own Money - Literally!

This will be a trip down Memory Lane
for anyone over 50 years old at the time of writing

Before 1971, there were not 100 pennies to the pound. For over a thousand years, a pound had been divided into twenty shillings (now 5p) and a shilling was worth twelve pennies, making 20 x 12 or 240 pennies in the pound.

Even before Brimscombe port was built, the owners of the canal were experiencing a problem with these figures. The Government of the time was too concerned over the Napoleonic wars with France to be bothered with making copper coins and the teams of navvies, paid with a large coin and told to divide it up among themselves, couldn't do so. There weren't enough copper coins to go round. Maybe this was one of the causes of trouble in the *Ship Inn*?

Big businesses came to the rescue by issuing their own coins. All over the country, these coins, known as 'tokens' were used instead of proper money. The Thames & Severn Canal Company went down this route and bought three tons of copper to make 309,000 of its own halfpennies. Though not recognised as legal money they entered the local currency and, when a trader had collected 480 tokens, he or she could exchange them at the port offices for a real sovereign or pound.

With so many made, tokens still turn up today, not just in this country but all over the world. Most of them are well worn but this is a sign that the tokens were much used and therefore trusted.

By 1818 the coin shortage had eased and, along with other tokens, Parliament banned the use of Thames & Severn halfpennies. However, banks could still issue their own paper money, (as Scottish ones still do) and, in the same year that tokens ceased to be used, a local boat owner and carrier, Richard Miller, issued his own bank notes. Unfortunately, his Brimscombe Port Bank went bust in 1822 and all that remains is a one guinea (£1.05) note, now in the Gloucester Record Office.

The Severn trow on the token was adopted as the Cotswold Canals Trust logo. The words 'Thames and Severn Canal' appear around the edge, while the date is found under the boat, in Latin numbering, MDCCXCV (1795). It is worth keeping a lookout for tokens with a striped sail on the trow. It is thought that only ten of these were

made before the die broke so, while an ordinary token is worth a few pounds, one with a striped sail is worth hundreds, if not thousands, of pounds. The image on the reverse side is recognisable as the eastern entrance to Sapperton tunnel at Coates.

How this one guinea note survived is a mystery. Scribblings on the back suggest it had even been used for scrap paper at some time. There's one bit of handwriting found on the front too. In this case, Richard Miller actually signed the note by hand after he promised 'to pay the bearer on demand the sum of one guinea.' Not the happiest of autographs to survive.

Wooden Boat Building

A list of lock details recorded in the 1780s reveals an oddity. All the locks from Wallbridge in Stroud to Brimscombe are about 69 feet long and 16 feet wide, the size necessary to accommodate Severn trows. Beyond Brimscombe, to the Thames, they are all about 91 feet long and a few inches under 13 feet wide, ideal for Thames narrow boats. So which sort is Bourne lock, the first one upstream from Brimscombe? As our pupils who measured it can confirm, it is:

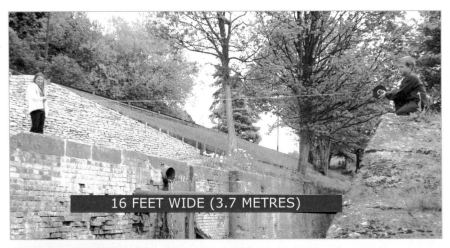

16 FEET WIDE (3.7 METRES)

90 FEET LONG (27 METRES)

It was both and neither. The lock is the length of those at the Thames end but the width of the Severn end, able to handle either sort of boat, but why build it when Brimscombe Port was designed to make such a lock unnecessary?

The reasoning behind this unique lock lies with a feature found on old maps but no longer visible today. There were a couple of dry docks just beyond the lock. Here boats were built and, when finished, the dock gates, hinged at the bottom, were dropped flat onto the canal bed allowing the boats to float out. Narrow boats could head into the port or east to the Thames while, thanks to the extra-wide Bourne lock, trows could head west. It was also possible for boats of either size needing repair to be able to enter the dry docks. Once in, the dock gates were lifted and water drained out, down a conduit into the Frome.

The docks were in use until the 1920s but became pointless once the canal closed in the 1930s. During the 1960s the local angling club decided to adopt them. They should have made checks before they flooded them and something went wrong. Rats, or possibly water voles, had tunnelled beyond the walls into one of the Critchley buildings. The morning after the docks were filled, workers turned up to find their part of the factory under water. No more was heard of the angling club's ambitions. For some years, the dry docks decayed and were eventually filled in.

The canal company owned its own boats for a time and used the dry docks at Brimscombe to build them. In 1786, the first two narrow boats, aptly named Severn and Thames, were launched and soon new improved boat designs left the docks. So much improved were they that, as early as the 1790s, Thames boat builders started to copy them.

The dry docks shortly before infilling.

17

A new style of boat, a salt barge, was also built at the Bourne. Because it was 65 feet long and 12 feet wide, it could pass through either sort of lock. A boat of similar proportions was built to be towed by trows up to Brimscombe and from there it was towed by Thames boats to London, avoiding the need to unload cargo from one boat and reload it onto another.

Not content with modifying Thames boats, a new trow was developed, one capable of going beyond the Severn and out to sea. The snag was literally the keel. This embedded in sand banks on the Severn and, once caught, a boat could break up. There again, without a keel, a boat is hopeless at sea. The Brimscombe-built trows had a keel for travelling in the Bristol channel to South Wales but it could be removed when the boat entered the Severn estuary.

Most of these boats have long gone but the Severn, which was influential in their design, was also responsible for preserving just a few on its beach, about 20 miles from Brimscombe. This all came about because the Severn, with the second highest tidal rise in the world, was eroding the thin stretch of bank between itself and the Sharpness canal at Purton. In order to protect the canal, old boats were run aground at high tide and holes knocked in them to stop them floating away. Hundreds of thousands of tons of material washes up and down the river every tide and silt soon filled the boats to create a new bank. Between 1909 and 1963, over 80 boats were beached, making the site the biggest boat graveyard in Britain. There are guided tours at weekends. Search the internet for 'Purton Hulks' to find out more.

In the late 1800s, a totally new and different family of boats was built downstream from the port, at Hope Mills. However, we are getting ahead of ourselves so more about them later.

Opposite from the top: One of Paul Barnett's guided Sunday afternoon tours of the 'Purton Hulks' where some of the Brimscombe boats ended up.

Two ends (characteristically both bows) of the largest Stroudwater towed barge, The Envoy, now embedded among the Purton Hulks.

The Palace, a trow built in Brimscombe in 1823 was one of the first to have a moveable keel. This photo dates from about 1900 and shows how long-lived such boats could be. The background is Clevedon, way down the tidal Severn, a feat no trow could ever have performed without a moveable keel.

Road & Rail Rivals

1815 is famous for the Battle of Waterloo. Probably of more significance to Brimscombe folk was the construction of a turnpike road, from Stroud to Cirencester, known these days as the A419. As John Taylor had surmised nearly 200 years earlier, horses could pull many times as much using a canal boat than they could using a cart on a road and the process required fewer men. The new road then was unlikely to be a competitor for the canal. Rather it would only make distribution of goods easier.

Similarly, when the Stroudwater Canal was crossed by the then Berkeley, now Gloucester & Sharpness, Canal in 1828, it was seen as an asset, removing the need to negotiate the treacherous tidal sand banks of the River Severn. The Stroudwater Canal had to be raised by several feet where the two canals crossed but, otherwise, it was a good thing, particularly in the 21st century. Now that the Cotswold Canals are being restored, they will eventually join up with the Gloucester & Sharpness Canal to be part of the national waterway system.

Whilst the road and waterway links could be good for trade, another new form of transport was appearing, also good for trade but not for canals. It first appeared when the Sapperton tunnel was being dug. Some of the contractors used a primitive wooden railway to carry material in the tunnel. This novel transport soon came to the attention of the Thames & Severn Canal directors.

A note in the proprietor's book of October 1824 shows them considering building a railway from Saul Junction and they planned to run it parallel to the Stroudwater Canal in order to by-pass it. The idea was to avoid paying what were believed to be excessive charges to the Stroudwater Canal Company. Rail branches to Nailsworth and other villages were mooted too. Such a railway could be used by horse drawn carriages but an innovative alternative noted was a 'locomotive steam engine'. Had it happened, Stroud could have seen one of the first railway lines in the world passing through.

In the end, the Stroudwater Company lowered their charges and the Thames & Severn Company dropped their railway idea. The reason was that another railway line was threatening both of them.

The London and Birmingham Railway wanted to buy both canals, drain the water and lay their own railway line along the old canal bed. Oddly enough, the canal was saved by another railway company, The Great Western. The canal company could have sold out to the L and B and made a profit but the GWR stopped all that when the directors slipped the Thames & Severn Canal Company £7,500 not to accept the offer.

So, the Great Western preserved the canal for another century and constructed its own line throughout the early 1840s. This line was supposed to come through the Golden Valley at a gradient of 1:330 but, under pressure to watch construction costs, Brunel used a gradient of 1:60. It meant a shorter tunnel higher up the valley but the terrain along the side of the hills was not ideal. Alternate cuttings and viaducts were needed. The viaducts were built like wooden trestle tables, using Russian birch. It didn't work and they soon had to be replaced with brick.

A quirky effect of this can be seen today. The brick viaducts were wider and the corner of Bourne Mill had to be knocked out and rebuilt to fit the viaduct in. The roof of the mill now overhangs the viaduct.

Initially, the clerks at Brimscombe Port recorded trade increasing through the 1840s into the 1850s, as goods were supplied for railway construction. Inevitably though, the trains, being quicker, took trade away over the years which followed. A possible answer to this problem of falling trade came in the 1860s, a repeat of the London and Birmingham offer of the 1830s. This time, it was the Midland Railway Company who wanted to buy the canal and turn it into a railway line. With a gauge of 4' 8½" it could get two sets of lines along the canal and even through the Sapperton tunnel. The gradient was a manageable fraction of the GWR line too.

The Midland Company did get their line as far as Stroud and really did fulfil the 1824 dream of a branch to Nailsworth, but their 'Thames and Severn' railway itself never did proceed. Today, most of what is left of the Midland Railway is the Stroud cycle trail.

Part of the Midland threat had been that it could connect to other lines in England, most of which used the same gauge. The GWR 7' 0¼" broad gauge was incompatible so the company soon saw the sense of replacing the track with the gauge which the rest of the country used. This also solved another problem. Brunel laid the sleepers along the rails instead of across them. Despite ties, the rails pushed apart and needed to be replaced. Again, another quirk of this remains. Walking along the canal towpath, there are several places close to the railway line where iron bars have been driven in to the ground to hold up banks or support markers. A close inspection shows what they really are - Brunel's original railway lines from the 1840s. They are recognised by their 'Top hat' cross section.

There remains one other link between the canal and the railway, one which carried on after the canal closed. Trains could not get from Brimscombe up the valley beyond Chalford. It was too steep. A little banker engine at Brimscombe Halt helped the train up the hill before running back to the halt to fill up with water from the canal to wait for the next train. After the canal closed, the railway carried on sourcing water from it by replacing the Beales Lock gates with a concrete dam in 1952, to keep the little banker engine supplied. The dam still works well but will be removed when the lock is restored. Coming back to the 1820s, instead of thinking about a railway, the canal companies should have considered a towpath.

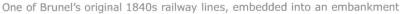
One of Brunel's original 1840s railway lines, embedded into an embankment

The Towpath

There wasn't a towpath west from Brimscombe. In fact, a letter in the County Archives, dated October 1799, reveals that a towpath was turned down as the advantages weren't considered worth the expense. Trows made the journey under sail or else a couple of men climbed out into the surrounding fields to pull them along. Both examples of these practices are seen in the picture on page 12. It took until July 1825 before the Proprietors' Minutes book considered a complaint about the missing path. There were some good arguments mentioned.

Firstly, a horse on a towpath could do the work of two men in a field without a path. Secondly, a boy and a horse had to stand around unemployed at Brimscombe, waiting for a man-hauled boat to return. This could take days. Thirdly, other canals had towpaths and horses and this was the only one without. It was breaking the link with other canals.

These and other arguments were backed by 24 signatures. It came late in the day but the canal finally got its towpath. Horses, however didn't use it for long. Something unique happened around Brimscombe when these fellows below appeared on the scene.

Donkeys

The traditional picture of an old canal boat usually features a horse-drawn affair. However, donkeys were the creatures that feature a lot in the Golden Valley and there are many old photos showing them delivering goods, especially around the narrow lanes of Chalford. Negotiating such narrow lanes with donkeys makes sense but why use them around Brimscombe Port?

The tradition is that Brimscombe people were light-fingered. The Port designers recognised this when they built an island with a drawbridge to stop people stealing the coal stored there, but it wasn't just coal at risk.

Bargees tethered their horses at night, only to find they'd gone walkabout by morning. Local farmers were reputed to be the culprits and the animals were said to have ended up pulling ploughs and carts instead.

The loss of a horse was a severe financial blow so the carriers looked for alternative animals, ones that could pull boats but not ploughs or carts. They chose donkeys or mules, the latter being milder natured. It is reported in Stan Gardiner's book, *The Stroudwater and Thames and Severn Canals In Old Photographs*, that two donkeys could pull a 70 ton barge between them.

The donkeys proved to be intelligent creatures too. Mike Mills tells the story of his grandfather, as a boy, working on a boat which reached the Sapperton tunnel. The men were going to 'leg' the boat through the tunnel while he was told to meet them with the donkeys at the other end. *"I don't know the way"*, he protested, only to be told, *"Follow the donkeys"*. The animals set off at their own pace, stopping where they fancied, but still arrived at the Coates entrance five minutes before the boat appeared.

The occasional lack of a towpath mentioned earlier also created difficulties when Smart's barges brought coal from Staffordshire to Brimscombe. There was never a towpath suitable for donkeys along the Severn around Gloucester.

The boats had to be towed at this point and the donkeys, instead of pulling the barge, had a ride instead - probably their favourite part of the journey.

This scene, taken near Ebley, shows some of the last donkeys to work the canal, sometime in the early 1930s.

This pair are unharnessed while their boat is taken through Bowbridge Lock. They are still yoked together.

The last picture shows a single donkey but does not show what the creature is pulling. The location is Ballinger's Lock at Chalford. Smart's Coal Merchants ran up to 30 boats from near here. That must have meant a lot of donkeys in the area, not all being used at once. What better use for an idle donkey than hire it out for deliveries? This may have been the reason behind Chalford having so many delivery donkeys. History has come full circle. Delivery donkeys are back. Who knows? Will we see them towing boats again one day?

Brimscombe about 1783

Thrupp Lane

Harrison's Mill

Dallaways House

Mr Peache's Mill

The Ship Inn

To Minching Hampton

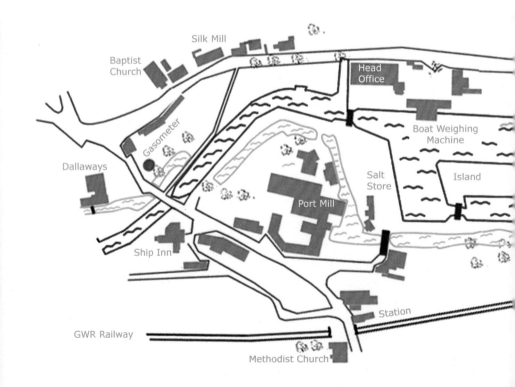

Silk Mill

Baptist Church

Head Office

Gasometer

Boat Weighing Machine

Dallaways

Salt Store

Island

Port Mill

Ship Inn

Station

GWR Railway

Methodist Church

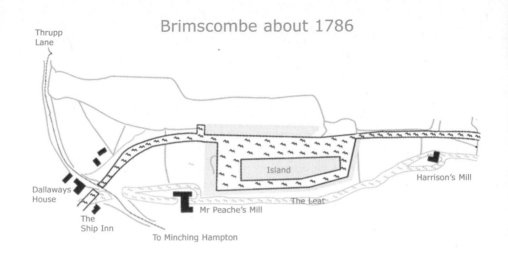

Brimscombe about 1786

Thrupp Lane

Dallaways House

The Ship Inn

To Minching Hampton

Mr Peache's Mill

Island

The Leat

Harrison's Mill

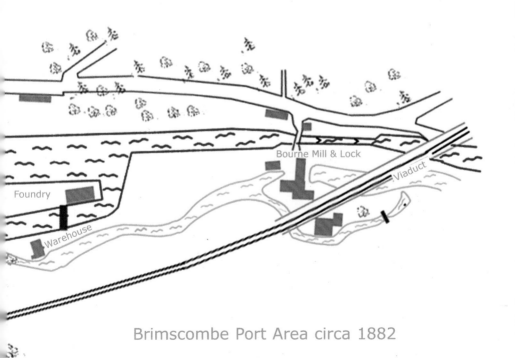

Foundry

Warehouse

Bourne Mill & Lock

Viaduct

Brimscombe Port Area circa 1882

Goods

Meticulous details about what the boats brought through Brimscombe Port are found in the County Record Office. They include foodstuffs such as cheese, cider, perry, hops, sugar, bread, carrots, butter, salt and grain. Other materials such as timber, flax, hides, tallow, oils and more general chemicals were unloaded along with metals like tin, iron and lead or alloys such as brass. Thousands of tons came into the port in the late 1700s, ten thousand of which were coal. The bulk of it came from the Staffordshire coal fields, while Forest of Dean coal made up some of it. The latter was more inferior but had less distance to come and was cheaper. Once trows were adapted to become sea-going vessels, more coal came from Newport in Wales.

One problem was that a lot of materials were only used locally and the canal beyond Brimscombe got little use. To make it worse, such boats as went on to London often had nothing to bring back, so no money was made on the return journey. Some bargees hung on in London for days, even weeks, hoping for trade. Meanwhile, complaints grew in Brimscombe about goods for London piling up while no boats came back from there to collect them.

The boat weighing machine

The canal company was also losing money in another way. It charged boat companies by the weight of material they brought into the port. Inevitably carriers tried all sorts of tricks to avoid paying where they could. The problem was solved by installing a weigh-bridge in 1844. It took the form of a submerged cradle that boats would sail onto and then the water was drained. The cradle hung on a beam that had weights on the other end.

The model of the boat-weighing machine

The mechanism was based on balancing a see-saw - clockwise moments equals anticlockwise moments for those studying physics at school. In practical terms, the weight on one side multiplied by the distance from the pivot is the same as the mass one the other side times the distance from the pivot on that side, when the see-saw balances. At Brimscombe Port, one ton sitting on the cradle holding the boat could be balanced by 24 pounds (approx. 10.5kg) at the other end.

The machinery and its housing cost £1,062, 15 shillings and sixpence in old money. It was worth it. In the following year, the machine revealed that the owners of the 688 boats weighed had tried to slip 1,267 tons of goods past the toll collectors. The money reclaimed on these items came to £153, 18 shillings and fourpence.

Within ten years the machine had paid for itself. It continued in use for another 90 years but in 1937, following the closure of the canal, the boat-weighing machine was dismantled. The area it occupied became a swimming pool and there are still folk around who remember swimming in it, before the council banned them from doing so. The machine has gone but there are more than old photos to tell us what it looked like. The model on which it was based is owned by Gloucester Folk Museum and is currently available for viewing at Stroud Museum in the Park. The picture above is used with their permission.

Stone

While coal made up the bulk of the port trade, most of it has literally gone up in smoke. Of lasting significance is the stone from quarries around Brimscombe. A note in the canal company records of 1842 showed that they dropped their charges on stone quarried around Brimscombe in order to compete on price with other quarries supplying the Great Western Railway. A later note from the same year reveals that the port authorities scrapped charges altogether for stone used for building the Houses of Parliament. This made the cargo cheaper to deliver and so local quarries won the contract to supply the Cotswold limestone used in this world-famous building. Most of the material came from Wallsquarry half way up Brimscombe Hill but some came from higher up on Minchinhampton Common. Were the canal company very generous or did anyone have a financial interest in the success of the quarries?

Two sorts of stone are found along this valley. The upper layer around the common is known as weatherstone, probably due to its tough nature. It is attractive to look at, due to its rich fossils content, and it forms natural blocks. Lower down the hillsides the stone has hardly any fossils and is made of tiny spheres called ooliths

(Oo = egg, lith= stone - they look like small fish eggs). This is less weather resistant but is excellent for carving. It can be sawn by hand freely in any direction, giving it the name freestone.

The census records from Victorian times show the population of Brimscombe to be mostly poor labouring-class people. Some of them were quarry workers and may have been those who cut Parliament's building blocks. Their dwellings were humble but they were built from the exact same rocks that made our Parliament building. Most people in Britain have never heard of Brimscombe but whenever the Palace of Westminster appears on television, people around the world unknowingly see something of Brimscombe.

We are grateful to David Drew (M.P. for Stroud at the time of writing), for taking these pictures of how Cotswold stone was used in the Houses of Parliament. The first picture reveals how detailed the carving can be. The marble statue in the second is nothing to do with the Cotswolds, but look at the background of beautiful carved stones. They came from here. A fitting tribute to the canal company, which helped secure the contract to transport the Brimscombe stone to Westminster, is found in a handwritten note at the end of one of the canal repair books. It informs us that the last boat through the Sapperton tunnel in 1904 carried a cargo of stone.

A Century Later

'The little hamlet surrounded by woods', of 1779 had changed dramatically in a hundred years, thanks mostly to the port. A comparison of the 1783 map with the one of 1882 shows how much development had occurred. The maps can be found on the centre pages (26 & 27). Two major new routes through the village stand out. First was the new road which is now better known as the A419. The second route is the railway line. Already it was taking trade away from the canal, which had ceased to make a profit.

Brimscombe had its own railway station at the entrance of the tunnel running beside the Methodist Church, reputedly the shortest railway tunnel in the world. This expensive break in the cutting was because folk feared the bank would collapse, landing the Methodist Church on the railway line. Whether this would have happened or not, people in the church today can still feel the whole building shake every time a train trundles past.

The other more modern feature was the gasometer. This stored gas made from coal at Brimscombe's own gas works, situated near Wimberley Mill. It supplied many of the villages along the valley. Candles were becoming obsolete as they were replaced by gas lighting, while gas fires and street lights began to appear. The discovery of North Sea gas made the gasometer redundant in the 1960s and it soon became scrap.

The island still had a building on it, the foundry. Stocks of iron ore and coal were mined a few miles away in the Forest of Dean and further sources could be supplied by trow from the Midlands. Add to this the boat builders' needs for steel and there was plenty of work here. Most of the buildings erected during the 100 years between 1782 and 1882 were around the port. The best known at the time was the company headquarters, soon to become a school. Close to it was the weigh-bridge, followed by a scattering of other smaller outbuildings.

The buildings beside the old short stretch of Brimscombe Corner are still there but have changed their function. Gordon Terrace, now a row of shops, was a silk mill and the gables at the back were not originally there. Instead, a long flue ran up the hill to a chimney, on a site high enough for the wind to take the smoke away.

The Old Mission Chapel had been a Brethren Assembly, but was (erroneously?) labelled a Baptist Chapel on a map at this time.

Some mills were modified and the Port Mill acquired this curious little wedge shaped chapel, though memories are hazy about which church it belonged to and what sort of services went on there.

The so called 'East Wharf Cottage' is actually on the south side of the port opposite the foundry and is one of the few port buildings to survive. At present it is used by the Nelson Trust, named after the former public house up the hill where the charity started.

This early 20th century picture shows Henry Stevenson, the last wharfinger (worker on the wharf area) who lived in the West Wharf cottage with his wife and seven children until the port closed. The cottage was condemned and demolished in 1976. It would have a preservation order on it these days.

Next to the West Wharf Cottage was a salt store, pictured above about 1905.

Tradition has it that salt stored in the surviving building impregnated the walls over the years and one could taste the salt just by licking the walls. Rumour also has it that one still can. Care to try, anyone?

Steel Boats

In 1843 Brunel amazed the world by launching a steel boat which didn't sink, the *S.S. Great Britain*, now a museum in Bristol. This led to another form of Brimscombe boat-building, Edwin Clarke's steel boat enterprise a few hundred yards downstream from the port at Hope Mill. His steam-powered boats were driven by paddle wheels and propellers. The first was *Gordon*, named after General Gordon who had just been killed at Khartoum. Appropriately, the boat was dispatched immediately up the Nile to avenge this hurt to British pride. Along with later boats, the engines took up so much space that there was scarcely room for more than a crewman. Most likely, such small craft towed other boats.

Edwin Clarke died in his thirties and his works were soon taken over by Isaac Abdela, who had previously built boats in the Midlands. He ran into financial difficulties and pretended that a Mr. Mitchell had invested money in the company to keep it solvent. The newly named Abdela & Mitchell fooled its investors and carried on trading and even introduced a new invention, the diesel engine. Boats that were narrow enough went east, through the Sapperton tunnel to London and abroad. Bigger boats went west, down to the Severn. Some ocean-going ones had to be dismantled and packed as kits to be reassembled elsewhere.

These Brimscombe-built boats were used as pleasure craft on the Thames but were also important work horses carrying goods on rivers and lakes in places as far away as Africa and South America.

Most Brimscombe boats have long gone but a Clarke's one, *Mary*, can be seen among the Purton Hulks, if the odd exposed rivet protruding from the mud counts. Abdela and Mitchell boats may still be in use today in this country and a few of the thousands sold to South America likely remain at work. The boat which stars in the film *The African Queen* was reputedly built in Brimscombe and is thought to have ended up in Florida. Abdela's boat building company experienced further cash flow problems and, with no more fictitious Mr. Mitchell or Mr. anyone else to inject imaginary money, boat building stopped in 1921.

Opposite: A very strange sight in its day. A large steel boat under construction without a dry dock.

GORDON 1885

Opposite Above: Clarke's first boat, *Gordon*, moored in the Port.

Opposite Below: Most Clarke and Abdela boats were photographed on trials and many pictures survive in the Gloucester Records Office (filed under reference D5631). It is with their permission that the photos in this chapter are copied. Mr Abdela appears on almost all of them. His unusual name comes from his ethnic origins. He was a Sephardic Jew as is evidenced by his bushy beard. He used his race to his advantage. He enjoyed days off on both Jewish and Christian holidays.

Below: Unlike the previous boat, *Cliveden*, built in 1892, had room for passengers and goods, as well as the engine. It is moored in front of the salt store and the wharfinger's (wharf labourer's) cottage.

Education

At the time the Thames & Severn Canal was being built, most children did not go to school. There was a school in Thrupp at that time but this only had about 18 pupils. Most left at age seven, to work in the mills. Some got more education in the Sunday schools but many adults couldn't read, let alone write.

In Victorian times primary schools became compulsory and secondary ones began to appear. In 1890, the port manager's house became a polytechnic and by 1899 it had 453 students. The conditions were not good and the attached warehouse was partitioned up and made into a more practical building. It was opened by the Duchess of Beaufort in 1911. It taught practical skills such as metalwork and woodwork to boys of 12 years through to adults, both during the day and at evening classes.

It was renamed Brimscombe County Secondary School in 1949 and there are many stories of life there, especially concerning the strict discipline. The stories include badly behaved boys being made to walk the plank into the port whilst seriously difficult lads were marooned on the island to give the teachers a break. All this when there was a dangerous giant pike in the water too ...

It's been difficult to pin down the facts behind these legends and, no doubt, there has been embellishment with time. However there are still many reminiscences around and they deserve a whole book to themselves. It was the end of an era when the school closed in 1962 and pupils transferred to Manor School, Eastcombe, now Thomas Keble.

Opposite Above: A metalwork class, thought to be about 1910. How does it compare to today's school environment and lessons?

Opposite Below: A collage of photographs taken at the re-opening of the much-improved Brimscombe Polytechnic. The Duchess of Beaufort performed the honours on 5th October 1911.

RE-OPENING OF BRIMSCOMBE POLYTECHNIC BY THE DUCHESS OF BEAUFORT, OCTOBER 5th, 1911.

1. Exterior of Polytechnic after improvements (from north-east side). 2. Interior central hall. 3. The Duchess being received at door. 4. The Duchess leaving the Polytechnic. 5. The Duchess formally opening building by unlocking the doors.

Decline, Closure & Decay

Even before the canal was built, Robert Whitworth, an expert in his field, described the ground beyond Chalford as the worst he'd come across. The route was notorious for leaks and, for over a century, water had to be pumped into the canal by a steam engine at Thameshead, in order to keep the summit levels topped up.

Bargees sometimes had to unload cargo to float clear of the canal bed in shallower patches. Frustratingly, once they had cleared the shallows, they needed to unload what they still carried in order to return to collect what they had left behind. Once back with that, they needed to reload the second cargo before they could continue through deeper, more manageable, water.

At other times, a single load had to be spread across three boats to avoid running aground. By the 1890s the canal became unusable beyond Chalford and there wasn't the money for repairs. The County Archives have a letter to the authorities at this time, written by Edwin Clarke. He complained that his boats couldn't get through the tunnel to the Thames so they had to take a route via the Severn, Bristol and the Kennet & Avon Canal, adding several days to his delivery schedules and pumping up his costs. The County Council stepped in during 1901 but were soon to regret their £5,000 estimate for repairs which reached £25,000 by 1905. The job still wasn't done by this stage and clearly wasn't going to be done. Already the last boat had passed over the summit. Lower down though, Brimscombe Port kept working with coal and other materials coming in. The foundry on the former coal island continued to flourish and boats continued to be made. Nevertheless, during the 1920s, the Thames & Severn was struggling to compete with the road and rail links passing alongside. On 9th June 1933, the canal closed.

The Stroudwater survived through the Second World War but that route, from Severn to Stroud, ceased to function in the 1950s. What followed, for the last half of the 20th century, has been a tale of loss posing as progress.

It wasn't long before the hump-backed bridge had to be removed because it had become impractical for loaded buses. They were prone to bottoming out on it, ending up as see-saws with their drive wheels spinning helplessly off the ground, a problem unknown in the days of horse drawn traffic.

Above: Brimscombe Bridge seen from the Port with the *Ship Inn* on the left. Note that there is a path on both sides on the canal.

Below: The same bridge with the *Ship Inn* on the right.

The weighing machine, after a century of service, was now defunct so was sold for scrap, the space it left remaining as a swimming pool.

The closure of Brimscombe Poly in 1962, removed the last reason for keeping the former Thames & Severn Canal Company Headquarters. In fact, it was in the way. The A419 at the time ran almost exactly on the same line and at the same width as it had been when it was built in 1815. It swung round at a difficult angle behind the old port offices. Brimscombe corner was a lot narrower and tighter than it is today. The powers of the time decided that the only way to widen the road was to demolish the old building.

In a matter of days, Samuel West's warehouses and the port office manager's house with its beautiful spiral staircase were pushed into the port, which was then concreted over and modern factories built on the site. Only two pillars were rescued. The son of the owner of Bensons factory saved them as a feature in his garden.

About this time Dalaways was demolished. The reason for destroying this Tudor building, possibly the oldest in Brimscombe, beggars belief. It had been allowed

The demolition team at work on the boat-weighing machine

Brimscombe Polytechnic during demolition to make way for a realigned road.

Dallaways is the building nearest the camera photographed from Brimscombe Lane.

Above: Brimscombe Corner in the early 1930s.
Below: Brimscombe Corner today, following the demolition of the shops and other buildings to make way for the new road.

to decay and squatters had moved in. This priceless building was destroyed to make the squatters move on. It is now a derelict industrial site. with just a road named after it in Thrupp. Later buildings, on the south side of the A419, such as the Co-op and an electrical repair shop were cleared out of the way in the 1970s and the road widened. It seems hard to imagine that what is now the parking area outside Gordon Terrace was once a main 'A' road.

For almost 40 years, Brimscombe Port became an Industrial Estate. Bensons was the biggest employer, making ring binders. Boat building even reappeared with Simpsons, who reintroduced the Abdela and Mitchell brand name before they ceased trading in 2008.

Lately, so much of this has changed. Thanks to years of effort by the Cotswold Canals Trust and others, we are about to see the link between the Severn and Thames restored. Brimscombe Port will be reborn. At the time of writing we don't yet know what form it will take, but that will be another story!

Aerial photo of Brimscombe Port in 2006. The superimposed shading indicates the area originally covered by water (Photo courtesy Stroud District Council).

1 Port Mill
2 Salt Warehouse
3 Site of Canal Co. HQ
4 Site of boat weighing machine
5 Site of island wharf
6 East Wharf Cottage
7 Bourne Lock

Cotswold Canals Trust

On 12th May 1972, a meeting was held in Stroud Subscription Rooms to investigate the feasibility of restoring navigation on the Stroudwater Navigation, from its junction with the Gloucester/Sharpness Canal to Wallbridge, Stroud. This resulted in the formation of the 'Stroudwater Canal Society' which soon became the 'Stroudwater - Thames & Severn Canal Trust'. In 1990 the Trust announced that it was to adopt a new name - the 'Cotswold Canals Trust'.

The Cotswold Canals Trust has a vibrant and ever increasing membership (around 5,500 in 2010). Regular monthly social gatherings, canal based events and a quarterly magazine - *The Trow* - enable members to keep updated on the progress of restoration and to enjoy the canals.

'Armchair Members' are most welcome but those who want to take a more active role can choose from a wide variety of activities. Some enjoy helping to crew a trip boat, others like to man the publicity unit around the country. Of course many members enjoy restoring and maintaining the canal itself.

Some volunteers have a wide variety of skills whilst others with no previous experience still have their part to play. Whatever the case, there is a place for anyone who wants to get involved with this exciting project.

Why not join? Application forms are available wherever you see the Cotswold Canals Trust volunteers. Otherwise, contact details are:

Phone	01453 755535
email	mail@cotswoldcanals.com
website	www.cotswoldcanals.com

The Cotswold Canals Partnership

Prince Charles made his second visit to the Cotswold Canals at the invitation of the Cotswold Canals Partnership - seen here by Coates Portal of Sapperton Tunnel.

The Cotswold Canals
LINKING THE THAMES AND SEVERN
Partnership

www.cotswoldcanalsproject.org

From 1972, steady progress towards restoration was made by volunteers. The project took a leap forward in July 2001 when British Waterways and national charity The Waterways Trust published a feasibility report which led to the formation of the Cotswold Canals Partnership. The aim of the partnership is to build on work achieved to date and deliver the full restoration of the Cotswold Canals. The members of the partnership are:

The Waterways Trust
Cotswold Canals Trust
Stroud District Council
South West Regional Development Agency
Gloucestershire County Council
Wiltshire County Council
Gloucestershire First
Gloucestershire Rural Community Council
Environment Agency
Gloucestershire Soc for Industrial Archaeology
Learning & Skills Council
Cotswold Water Park Society
Inland Waterways Association
South West Tourism
Co. of Proprietors of the Stroudwater Navigation
North Wiltshire District Council
Cotswold District Council.

Representatives from these organisations belong to a project board which meets regularly to steer the project.

Acknowledgments

So many folk helped with this book, it is difficult to know where to start and, sadly some may get left out. Whoever you are, you are all appreciated.

The main source of information for anyone researching the canal involved has to be Humphrey Household's book, *The Thames and Severn Canal*. There can hardly be a single document on the subject that doesn't have his fingerprints on it. After a gap of 20 years the book was released in a new edition in 2009.

The bulk of the photos came from Mike Mills' collection and, unless credited to others, come with his copyright. Mike has thousands of old photos and hundreds who attend his slide shows can vouch for what a fascinating raconteur he is. The picture of Dallaways came from Mr. Jones who obtained it when Merret's, the Stroud photographers closed. The snap of the Stevenson family outside the cottage came courtesy of a descendant of Jim Jellyman.

Many of the pictures featuring Brimscombe school children are the work of Liz Peters. She is a governor of the school. Liz gave hours of her time taking pupils to Gloucester Archives, Stroud Museum, the Purton Hulks and more. Several pupils helped at the archives, copied data, transcribed documents and helped with the maps.

Many local folk shared memories. They were too many to record in this small book. Sorry to leave you out. Perhaps someone reading this could undertake collecting these stories, especially those about the school, or maybe you know someone who can?

So many stories became real when we could handle the actual documents and maps, some going back 350 years. The help and patience of the staff at Gloucester Record Office and Stroud Museum was excellent - and that's just with me, never mind the children.

Graham Hobbs, May 2010